# LEARN BY STICKER®
## More Phonics

workman
• NEW YORK •

Workman Kids
Workman Publishing
Hachette Book Group, Inc.
1290 Avenue of the Americas
New York, NY 10104
workman.com

Workman Kids is an imprint of Workman Publishing, a division of Hachette Book Group, Inc. The Workman name and logo are registered trademarks of Hachette Book Group, Inc.

LEARN BY STICKER is a registered trademark of Hachette Book Group, Inc.

Design by Ying Cheng and Lourdes Ubidia
The 10 low-poly images in this book are based on illustrations by Ying Cheng.
Activity illustrations and line art by Lourdes Ubidia
Concept by Alisha Zucker
Text by Katie Campbell

Workman books may be purchased in bulk for business, educational, or promotional use. For information, please contact your local bookseller or the Hachette Book Group Special Markets Department at special.markets@hbgusa.com.

ISBN 978-1-5235-2394-8
First Edition May 2024

Distributed in Europe by Hachette Livre, 58 rue Jean Bleuzen, 92 178 Vanves Cedex, France.

Distributed in the United Kingdom by Hachette Book Group, UK, Carmelite House, 50 Victoria Embankment, London EC4Y 0DZ.

Printed in China on responsibly sourced paper.

10 9 8 7 6 5 4 3 2 1

# HOW TO LEARN BY STICKER

## 1. PICK YOUR IMAGE.
Sticker maps for each sea animal are in the front of the book. Which animal do you want to sticker first? It's up to you!

**Sticker map**

## 2. FIND YOUR STICKERS.
Sticker sheets for each picture are in the back of the book. Use the image in the top right corner of each sticker sheet to find the one that matches the picture. Both the sticker map and sticker sheet can be torn out of the book, so you don't have to flip back and forth between them.

**Sticker sheet**

## 3. READ THE WORDS!
Fill in the missing letters to complete each word inside the sticker map, using the drawings as clues. Say the word aloud. Then find the completed word on the sticker sheet. Each sticker matches only one space on the sticker map. Place each sticker in the matching space on the sticker map. Be careful! The stickers aren't removable.

**Finished picture**

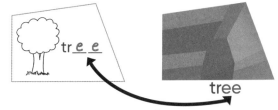

tr_e_ e_

tree

**Match**

## 4. TURN THE PAGE.
There are fun activities on the back of each picture to get extra practice and strengthen your phonics skills.

**Activity page**

**Activity answers**

# LET'S SOLVE AND STICKER!

# Directions

### Ending Consonants
Fill in the blanks using consonants to complete the words.

### Long e Sounds
Fill in the blanks with **e**, **ea**, **ee**, **ey**, **ie**, or **y** to complete the words.

### Final Blends
Fill in the blanks with the final blends **ld**, **lt**, **rd**, **rk**, or **sk** to complete the words.

### Long i Sounds
Fill in the blanks with **i**, **ie**, **i_e**, **igh**, or **y** to complete the words.

### Hard and Soft c Sounds
Fill in the blanks with **c**, **ck**, or **k** to complete the words.

### Long o Sounds
Fill in the blanks with **o**, **oa**, **oe**, **ow**, or **o_e** to complete the words.

### Hard and Soft g Sounds
Fill in the blanks with **dge**, **g**, **ge**, or **j** to complete the words.

### Long u and /oo/ Sounds
Fill in the blanks with **ew**, **oo**, **u**, **ue**, **ui**, or **u_e** to complete the words.

### Long a Sounds
Fill in the blanks with **a**, **a_e**, **ai**, **ay**, or **eigh** to complete the words.

### Diphthongs
Fill in the blanks using the diphthongs **ai**, **ea**, **oi**, **ou**, **ow**, or **oy** to complete the words. (A diphthong is two vowel sounds that make up one syllable.)

# MESSAGE IN A BOTTLE

Say the name of each picture.
Circle the **ending consonant** for each word.
Then fill in the letters to answer the riddle!

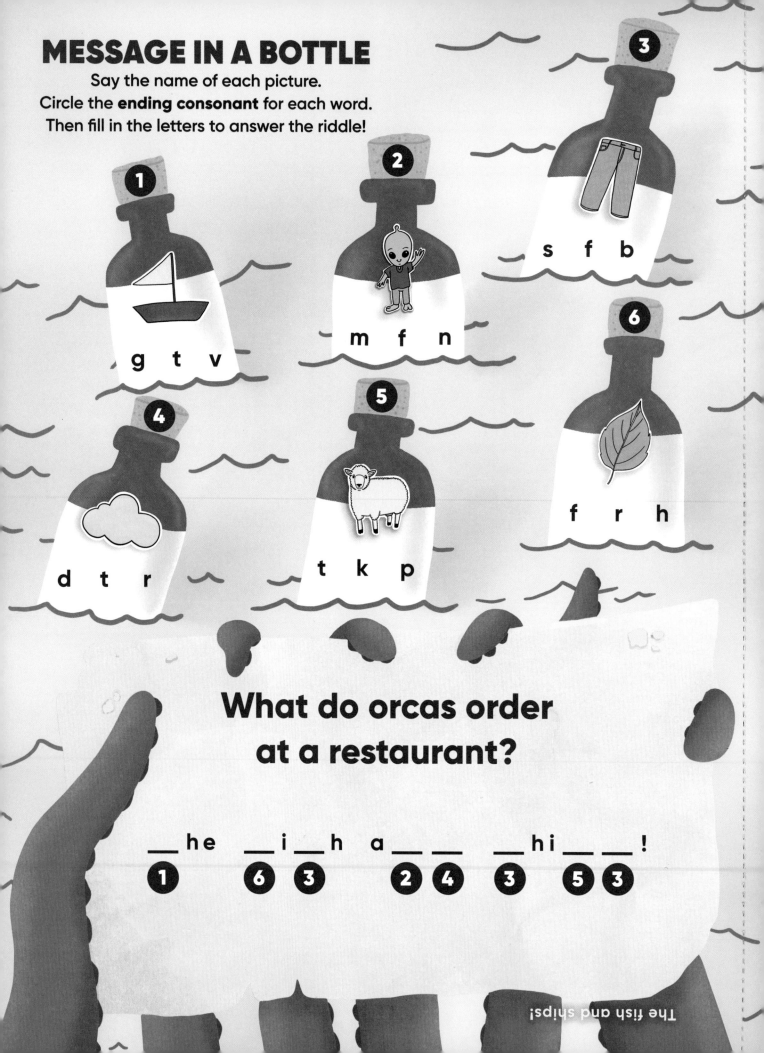

1. g  t  v

2. m  f  n

3. s  f  b

4. d  t  r

5. t  k  p

6. f  r  h

## What do orcas order at a restaurant?

__ h e   __ i __ h   a __ __   __ h i __ __ __ !
**1**      **6** **3**      **2** **4**   **3**  **5** **3**

The fish and ships!

# WORD BUILDING

Combine green letters with a pink **final blend** to make words.

sk

rk

a e i o

build

u m r

ld

d h w

c p s lt

b f n rd

an_le

dan_er

_a_e

_ent

mi_e

lo___

_omb

ra_e

hoo_

pen_il

_a_tus

ta_o

_ube

fen_e

so___

_ity

nap_in

du___

_ir_le

# CROSSWORD PUZZLE

Solve the clues to fill in the crossword puzzle.
Each answer has a **hard c** sound (as in *cup*) or a **soft c** sound (as in *mice*).

## Across:

1. There are eight c _ _ _ _ _ _ on my birthday cake.

5. Ballet, tap, and hip-hop are all types of d _ _ _ _ .

6. Milk and c _ _ _ _ _ is a popular breakfast.

7. Fly a k _ _ _ on a windy day.

## Down:

1. A cuckoo c _ _ _ _ makes a bird sound on each hour.

2. Hot sauce makes food taste s _ _ _ _ .

3. Superman wears a red c _ _ _ on his back.

4. Another word for coat is j _ _ _ _ _ .

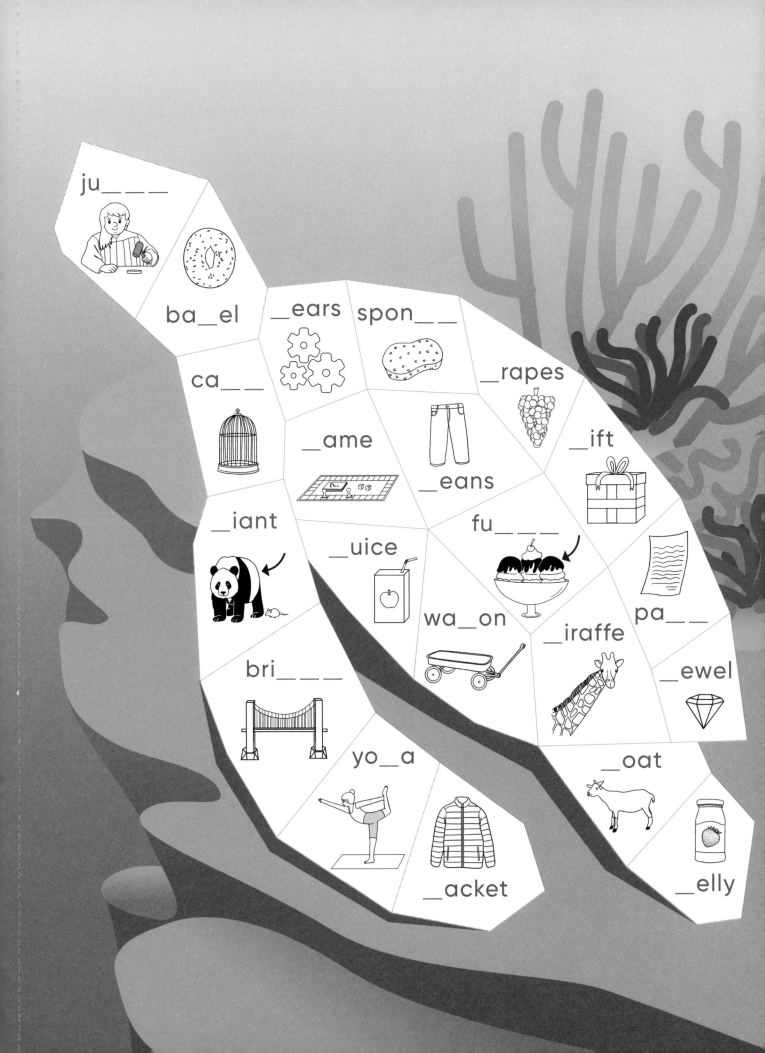

# TURTLE TALK

Say the word in each turtle shell out loud.
Sort each word into the correct column by sound:
**hard g** (as in *game*) or **soft g** (as in *giant*).

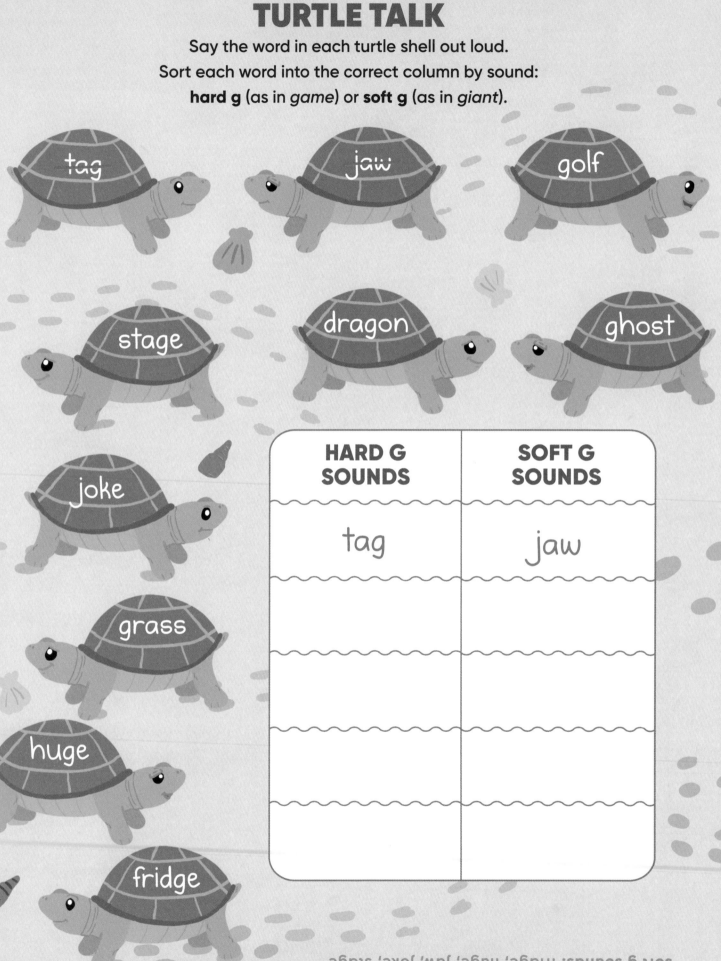

tag

jaw

golf

stage

dragon

ghost

joke

grass

huge

fridge

| HARD G SOUNDS | SOFT G SOUNDS |
| --- | --- |
| tag | jaw |

# RHYME TIME

Say the **long a** word in the box. Write rhyming
words with the given vowel combinations.

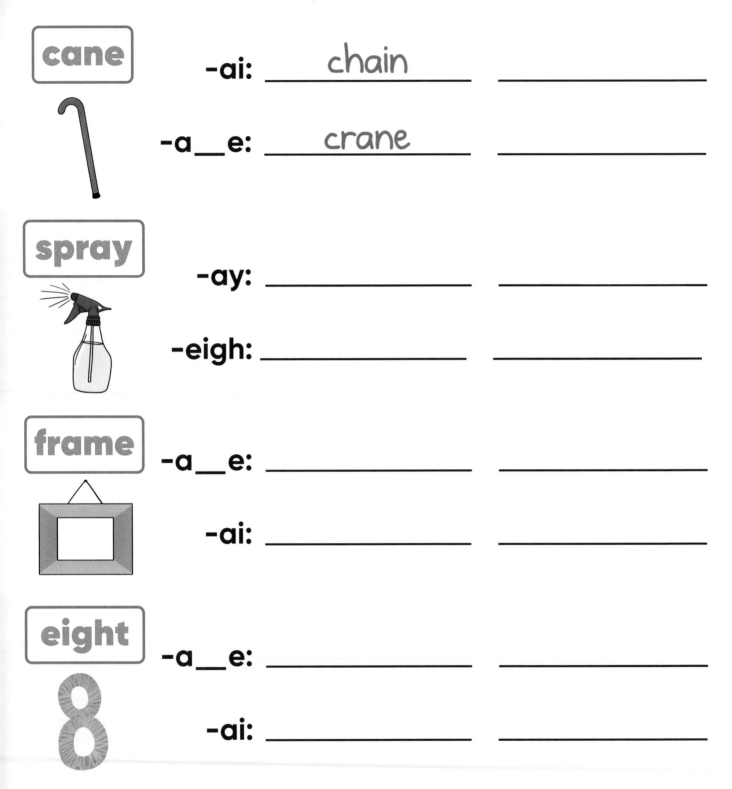

**cane**

-ai: _____chain_____ _____

-a__e: _____crane_____ _____

**spray**

-ay: _____ _____

-eigh: _____ _____

**frame**

-a__e: _____ _____

-ai: _____ _____

**eight**

-a__e: _____ _____

-ai: _____ _____

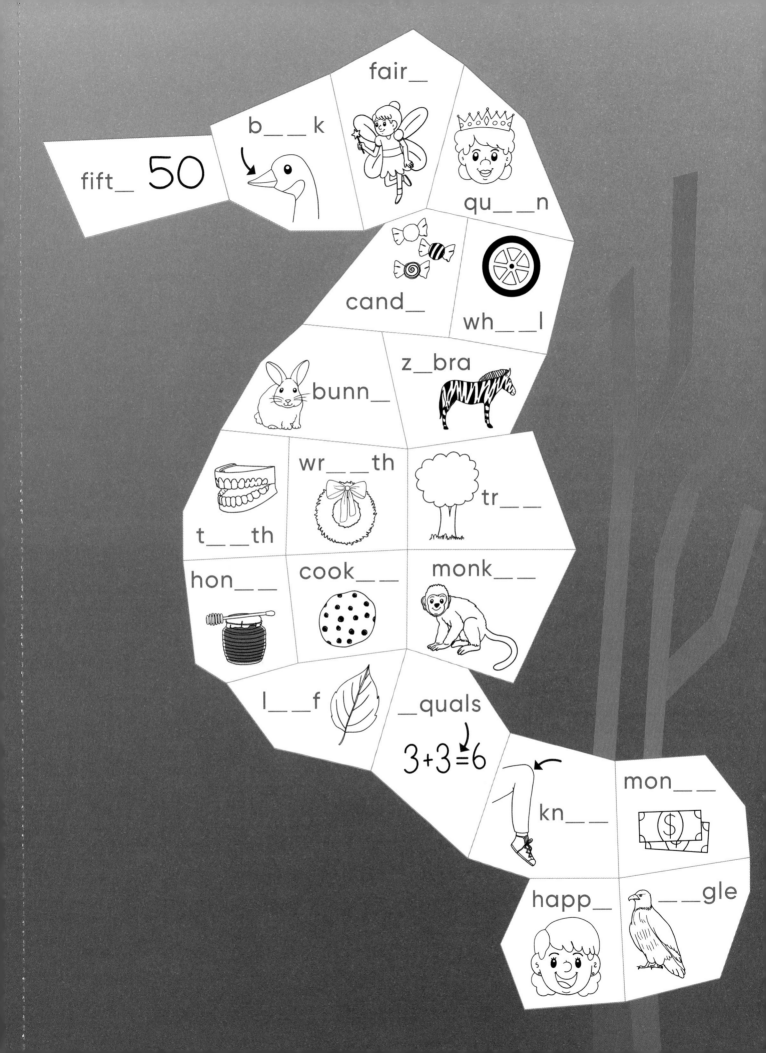

fift_ 50

b _ _ k

fair_

qu _ _ n

cand_

wh _ _ l

z _ bra

bunn_

wr _ _ _ th

t _ _ _ th

tr _ _ _

hon _ _ _

cook _ _ _

monk _ _ _

l _ _ f

_ quals

3+3 =6

kn _ _ _

mon _ _ _

happ_

_ _ _ gle

# WORD SCRAMBLE

Unscramble each **long e** word.
Then draw a line to the matching drawing.

l e b e t e

_____

k u t e r y

_____

n p u t e a

_____

n t w t y e

_____

o k o c e i

_____

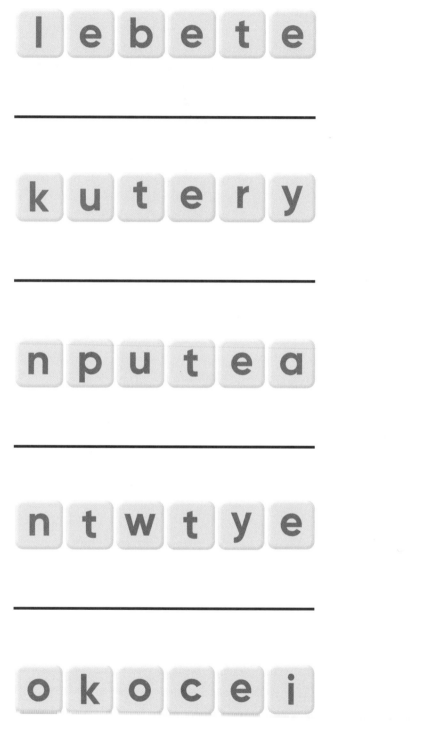

# WORD BUBBLES

Say the name of each picture out loud. Write the word that matches the picture.
If the word has a **long i** sound (as in *eye*), color the bubble orange.
If the word has a **short i** sound (as in *sit*), color the bubble green.

\_ \_ \_ \_ \_

\_ \_ \_ \_ \_ \_

\_ \_ \_ \_ \_

\_ \_ \_ \_ \_ \_

\_ \_ \_ \_ \_

\_ \_ \_ \_ \_

\_ \_ \_ \_ \_ \_

\_ \_ \_ \_ \_

# CROSSWORD PUZZLE

Solve the clues to fill in the crossword puzzle.
Each answer will have a **long o** sound.

## Across:

**2.** Another word for rock is _s_ _ _ _ _.

**5.** We drank hot _c_ _ _ _ _ on the snowy day!

**7.** Look out the car _w_ _ _ _ _ _ to see where you are going.

**8.** A _f_ _ _ _ is a baby horse.

## Down:

**1.** Bananas and lemons are both _y_ _ _ _ _ _ fruit.

**3.** The biggest bodies of water on earth are called _o_ _ _ _ _ _.

**4.** A word that means the same as "by myself" is _a_ _ _ _ _.

**6.** Kick the soccer ball into the _g_ _ _ _.

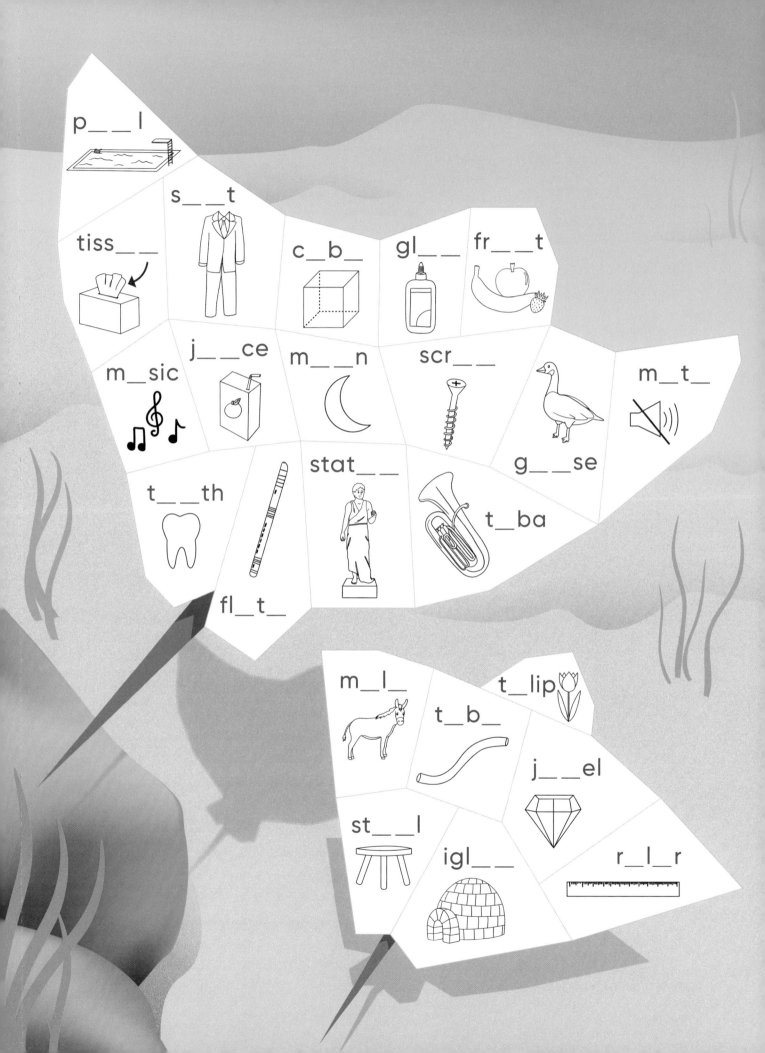

p_ _ _ l

s_ _ _t

tiss_ _ _

c_b_

gl_ _ _

fr_ _ _t

m_ _sic

j_ _ _ce

m_ _ _n

scr_ _ _

m_t_

t_ _ _th

stat_ _ _

g_ _ _se

fl_ _t_

t_ba

m_l_

t_lip

t_b_

j_ _ _el

st_ _ _l

igl_ _ _

r_l_r

# WORD SCRAMBLE

Unscramble the words—each has the /oo/
or **long u** sound. Then draw a line to the matching drawing.

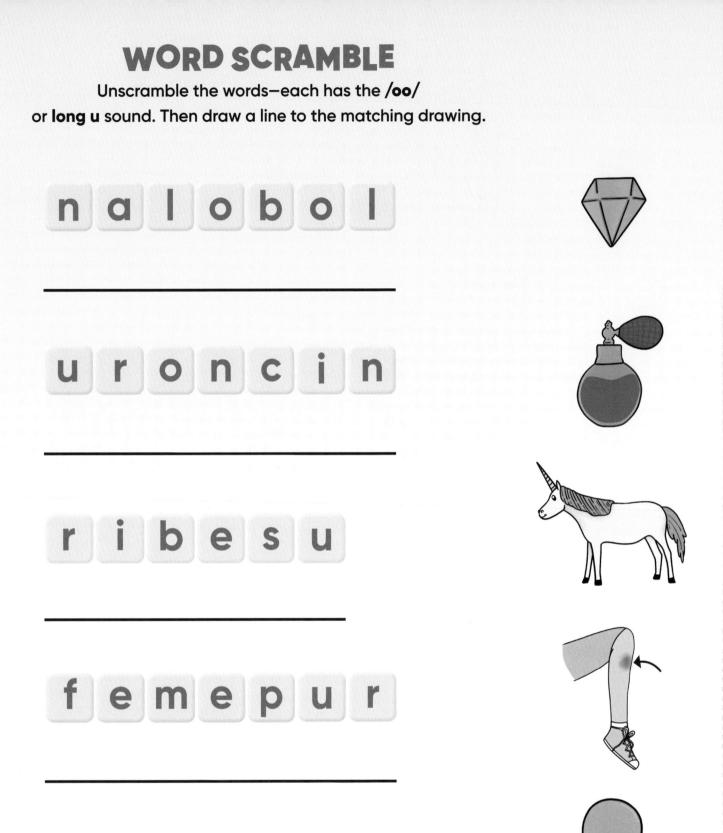

n a l o b o l

_____

u r o n c i n

_____

r i b e s u

_____

f e m e p u r

_____

e w e j l

_____

br___d

c___n

cl___d

fl___er

t___let

p___nt

c___

fr___n

b___r

t___s

b__l

___ster

p__r

b___

m___th

t__r

c___ch

h___r

m___se

ch___r

__l

# FISH FACTS

Read the clues in the clam shells.
Complete each word with the missing
**diphthong**: *ai*, *oi*, *ow*, or *oy*.

⭐ I can be forked, round,
square, or pointed.

⭐ I rhyme with *whale*.

⭐ Fish use me to move
through the water.

I am a t___ ___l fin.

⭐ I have orange, black, and
white scales.

⭐ I have the same diphthong
as in *shower*.

⭐ My name sounds like a
circus performer.

I am a cl___ ___nfish.

⭐ I am a type of shellfish.

⭐ I have the same diphthong
as in *ahoy*.

⭐ I can make pearls.

I am an ___ ___ster.

⭐ You can find me in
garden ponds.

⭐ I rhyme with *boy*.

⭐ I am a symbol of
luck in Japan.

I am a k ___ ___.

tail fin, clownfish, oyster, koi

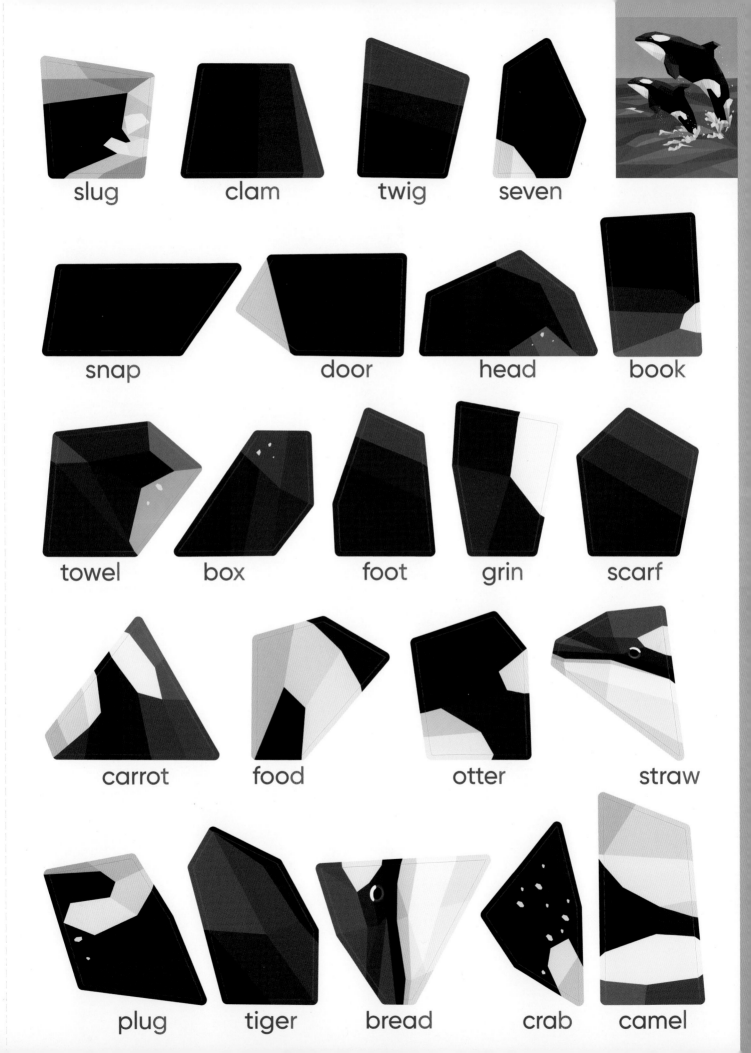

slug

clam

twig

seven

snap

door

head

book

towel

box

foot

grin

scarf

carrot

food

otter

straw

plug

tiger

bread

crab

camel

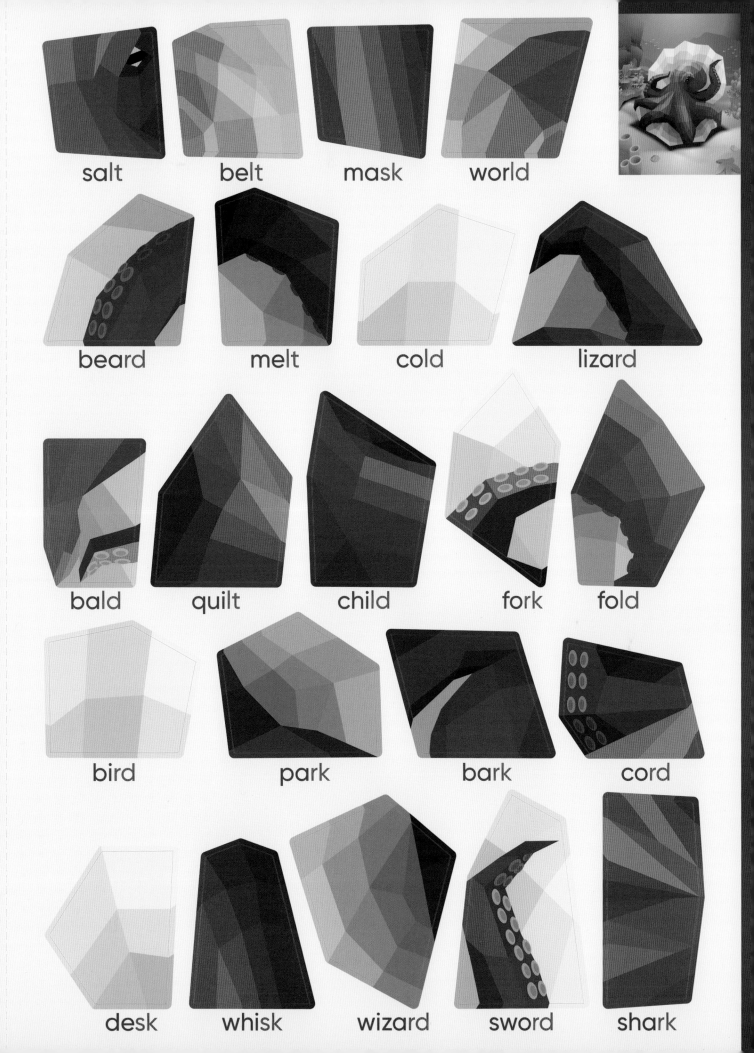

salt

belt

mask

world

beard

melt

cold

lizard

bald

quilt

child

fork

fold

bird

park

bark

cord

desk

whisk

wizard

sword

shark

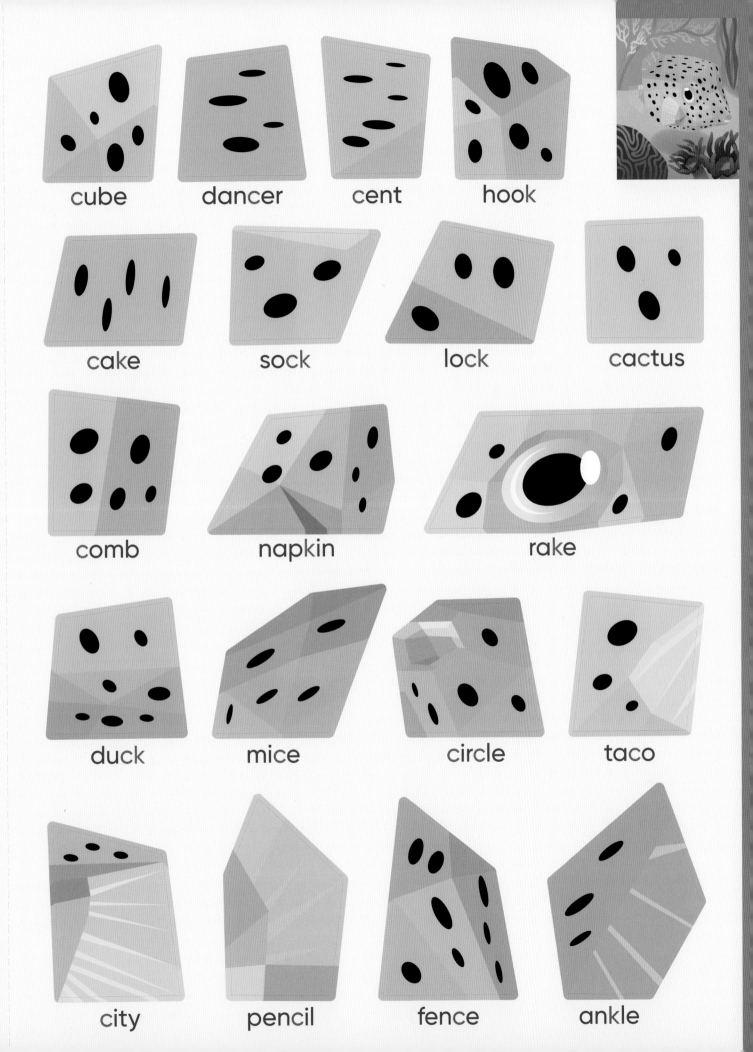

cube     dancer     cent     hook

cake     sock     lock     cactus

comb     napkin     rake

duck     mice     circle     taco

city     pencil     fence     ankle

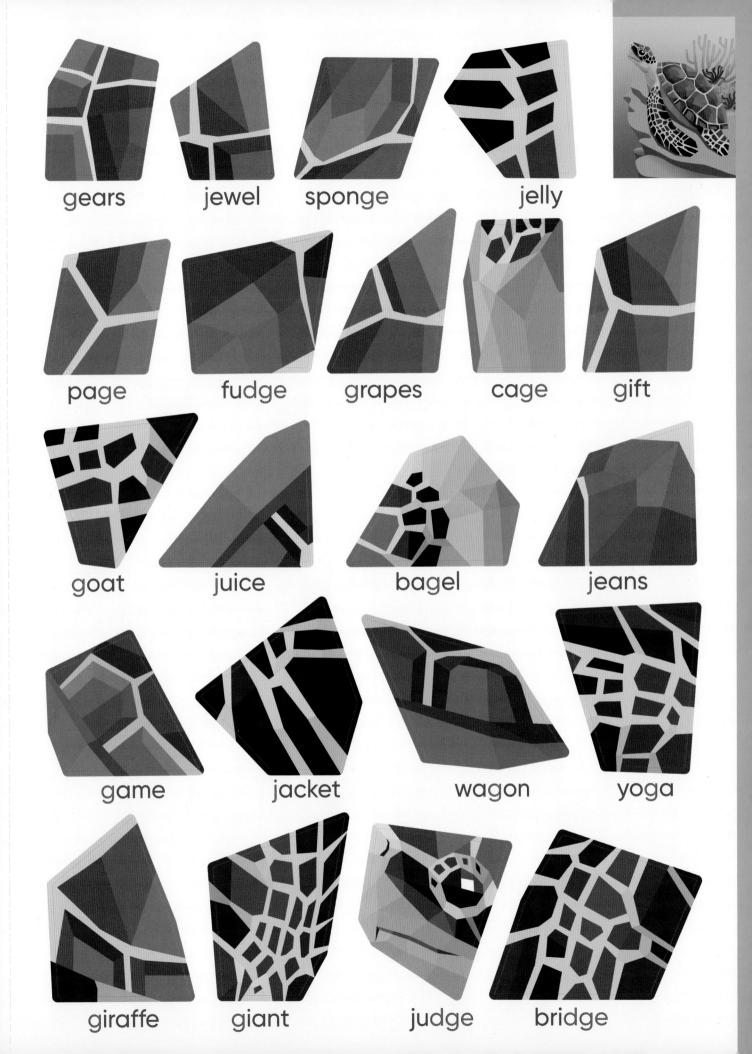

gears  jewel  sponge  jelly

page  fudge  grapes  cage  gift

goat  juice  bagel  jeans

game  jacket  wagon  yoga

giraffe  giant  judge  bridge

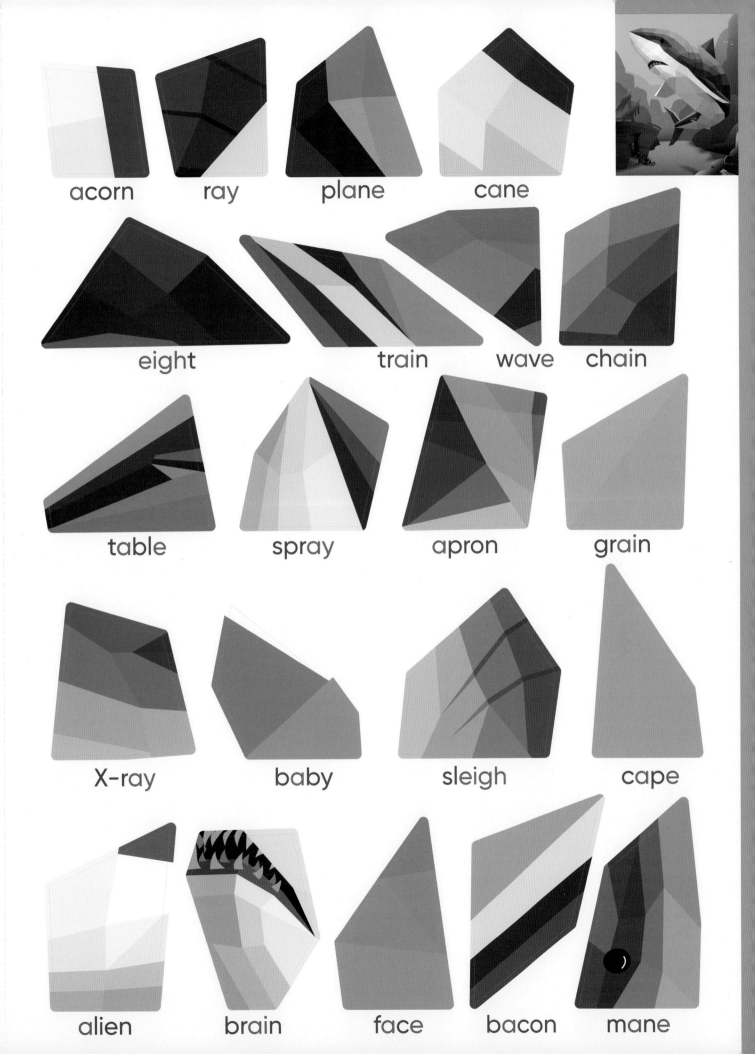

acorn ray plane cane

eight train wave chain

table spray apron grain

X-ray baby sleigh cape

alien brain face bacon mane

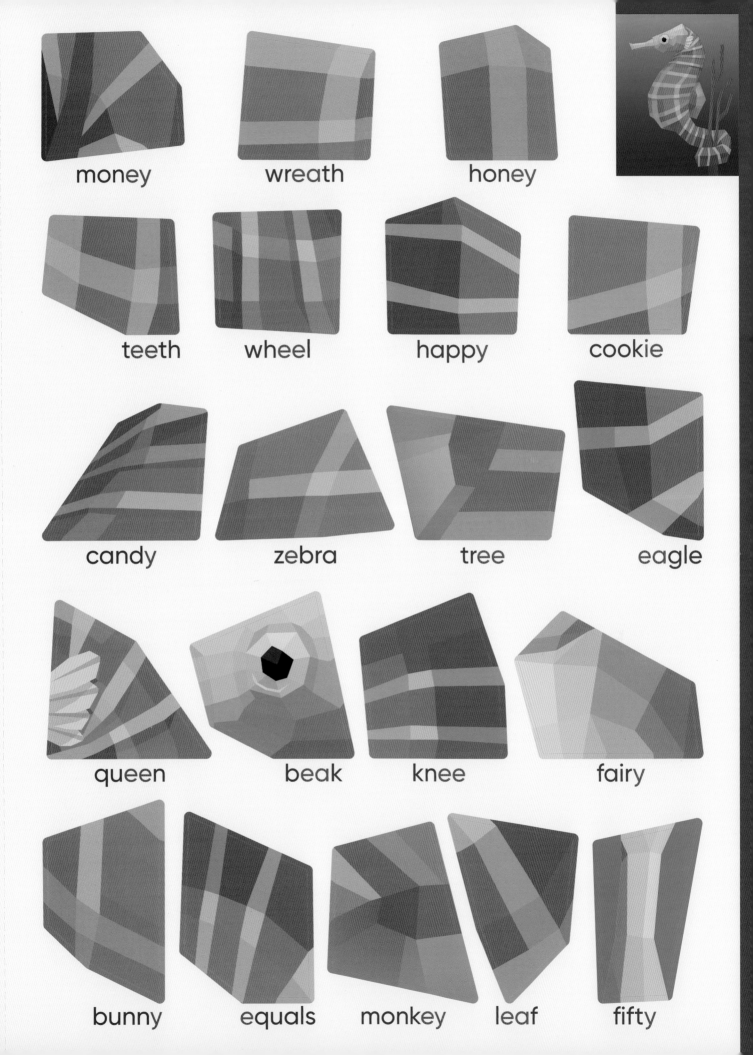

money

wreath

honey

teeth

wheel

happy

cookie

candy

zebra

tree

eagle

queen

beak

knee

fairy

bunny

equals

monkey

leaf

fifty

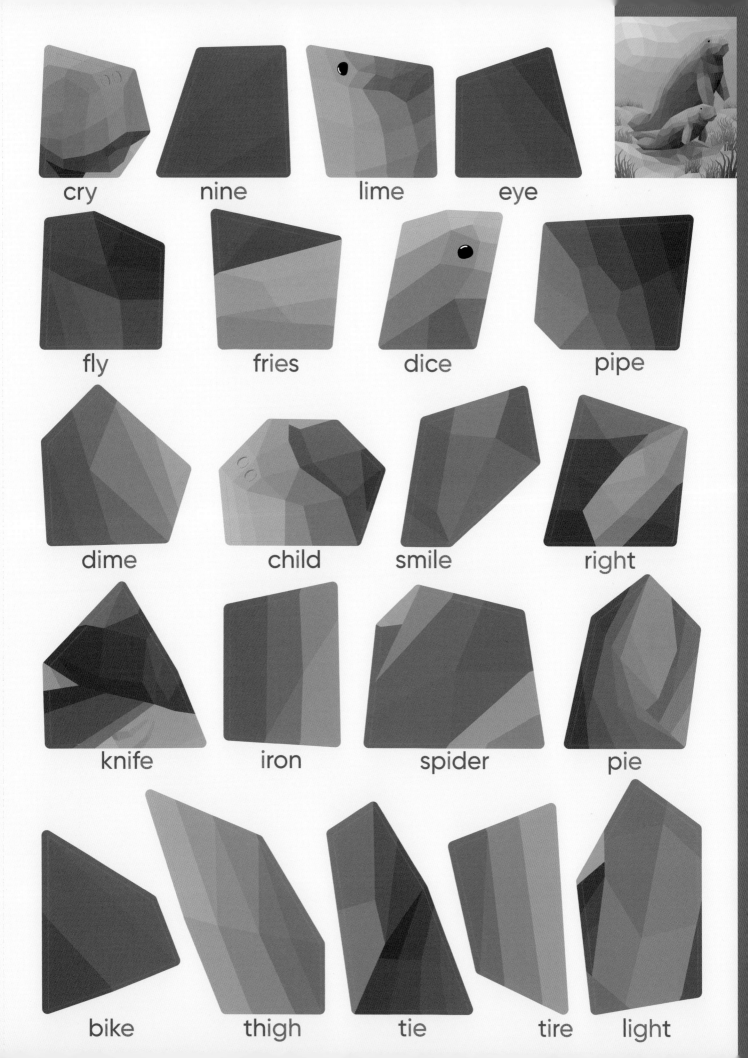

cry

nine

lime

eye

fly

fries

dice

pipe

dime

child

smile

right

knife

iron

spider

pie

bike

thigh

tie

tire

light

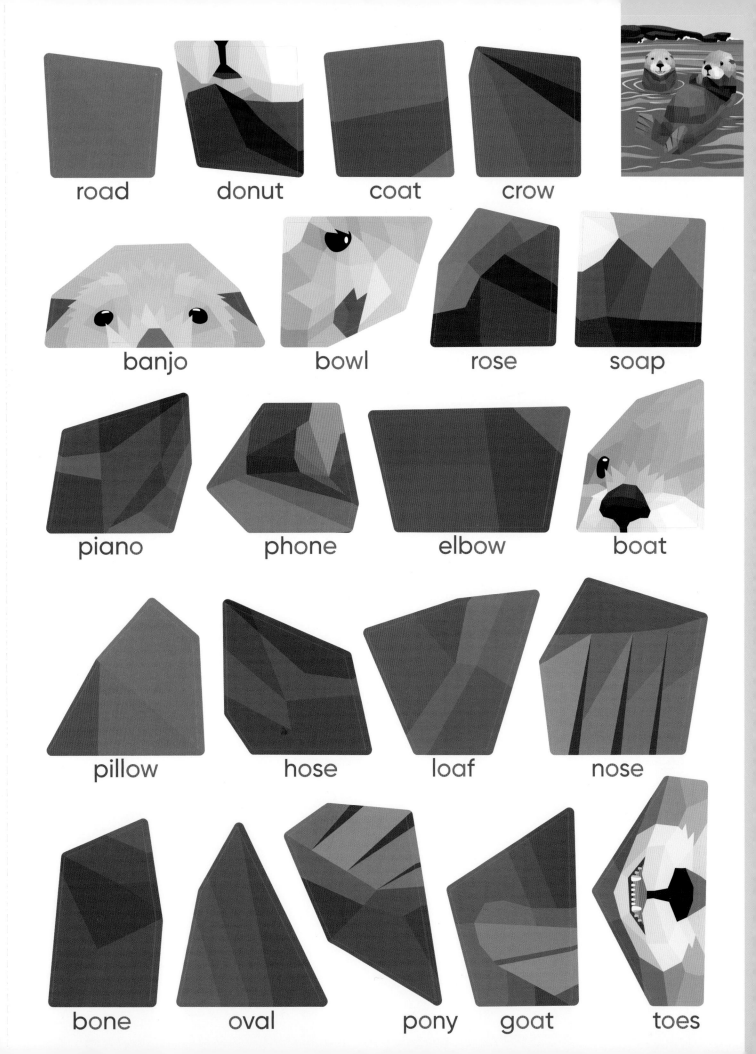

road     donut     coat     crow

banjo     bowl     rose     soap

piano     phone     elbow     boat

pillow     hose     loaf     nose

bone     oval     pony     goat     toes

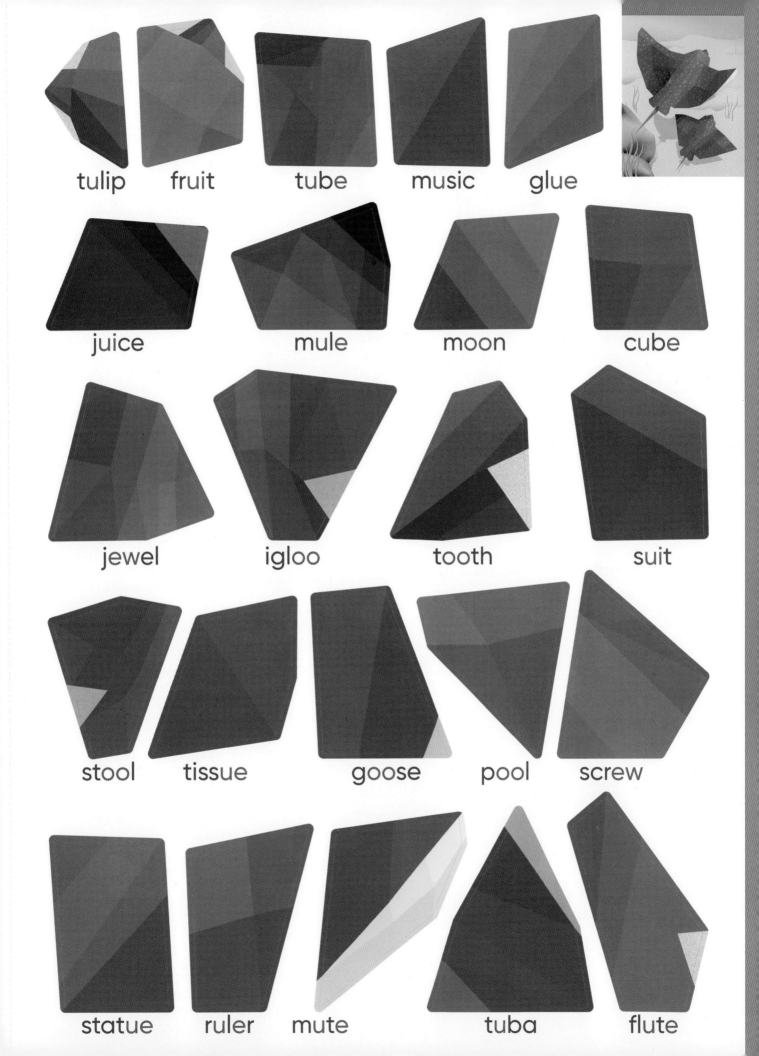

tulip    fruit    tube    music    glue

juice    mule    moon    cube

jewel    igloo    tooth    suit

stool    tissue    goose    pool    screw

statue    ruler    mute    tuba    flute

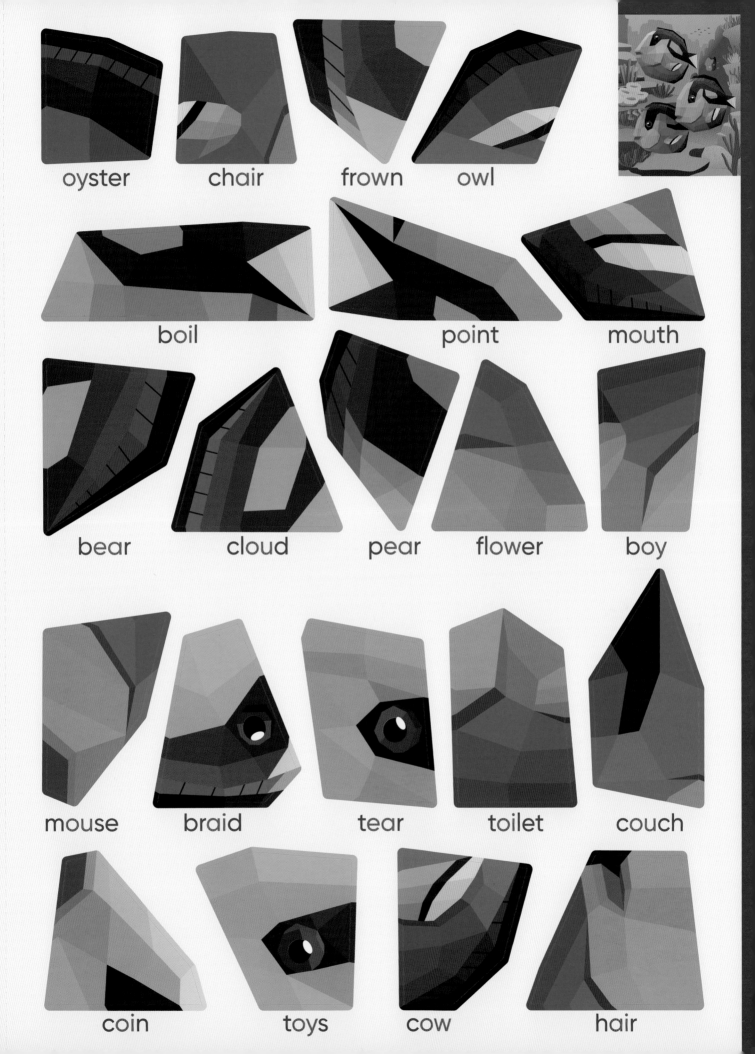

oyster    chair    frown    owl

boil    point    mouth

bear    cloud    pear    flower    boy

mouse    braid    tear    toilet    couch

coin    toys    cow    hair